POEMS
OF
LIFE

By

Michael L Skeet

Poems of Life

Published by Michael L. Skeet
23 Gresham Close
Gorleston-on-sea
Norfolk
NR31 7EA

The Author

Michael L Skeet was born in Great Yarmouth on 31st March 1949. Apart from his University years, he has lived and worked in and around the local area, although his hobbies of fishing, sports and his passion for life have taken him further a field. He has always embraced life's adventure.

Acknowledgements

My heartfelt thanks go out to all the people in life who have given me an insight into human behaviour, which has been an inspiration in the writing of these poems.

CONTENTS

THE WANTS OF LIFE

A friend asked me today,
"What do you want from life?"
I pondered
Then to answer this way.

I want to see, hear and touch,
because these things matter so much.
To talk and smell scented air
To feel the sun warming skin so bare.

I want a life that's full of passion
To wear any clothes despite the fashion
To give the joy that's deep within
To laugh if I want, or just to grin.

To fulfil a need with whom I choose
To gain, without first to lose
To run wild in the nude,
without people saying it's rude.

To look at the moon on a clear night
To take my love and hold her tight
To gaze at the stars that twinkle still
To question by chance or God's will.

To be with people who I call friend
Their image portraying the feelings they send
To know that somebody cares,
if at a time I need them there.

To keep within, a secret desire
One that sets my very soul on fire,
To pleasant memories of times past,
locked in my mind, forever to last.

Life is never simple, but always complex
To enjoy excitement, adventure and sex
To wear a twinkle in ones eye,
Not letting opportunity pass me by.

What is life? but a conception of ones mind,
that changes often from time to time
To see nature in all its glory
For life itself is a never ending story ………..

TRUE LOVE

Words could never express,
all your love and thoughtfulness
Your sparking eyes and smiling face,
makes my world a better place.

Don't blame me when I make you mad
Forgive me if I make you sad
I feel guilty when I make you cry
Without you dear, my love would die.

So simply to explain it all,
of happy memories I recall,
tender love that's always true,
deep in my heart,
Just for you.

SUMMER'S DREAM

As I lay and gaze up at a summer's sky
watching endlessly as the clouds drift by.
Their fluffy shapes appear to glow
forming faces of loves I know.

Down, down the lane of memories
of sweet fragrance and flowing trees.
Gentle breezes warm against my skin
increase the contemplative mood I'm in.

Floating away on forgotten dreams
of babbling brooks and rippling streams,
I hear your voice, such a lovely sound
ever softly, never loud.

With closed eyes and an inquisitive face
soon my heart begins to race.
Grasping out hopelessly at the image in my mind.
To return the moments time left behind.

But soon the clouds begin to disperse.
Gentle are the words of rhyme and verse.
For time, like the memory, slips away.
I awake to dream another day ......

HAIRCUT

Patiently in the barber's shop
waiting my turn to be cropped
Buzz Buzz Zip, the cutting sound
as swathes of hair fall to the ground.

"NEXT!"

> *" I haven't seen you for a while"*
> *as I sit down with a gentle smile.*
> *"No, I have been quite busy, given all"*
> *"Oh! A car knocked down the garden wall".*

"How's the family?" the barber asks
as he continues with his task.
"Norwich won this weekend" "got 3"
"Ah!" I replied, "did you see?"

> *"The weather of late has been dry and fine"*
> *"Yes indeed, for sometime"*
> *"The lawn I'm afraid is bloody scorched,*
> *and the ants are undermining the porch".*

Buzz Buzz Zip, more hair does fall.
"Hey! I didn't mean for you to cut it all"
"Oh sorry sir, I assure you it looks fine.
Anyway it will grow back in time"

> *There all done, mirror here, mirror there,*
> *Ankle deep in multi coloured hair.*
> *"Can I offer you anything else?"*
> *"No keep the change for yourself".*

Out once more into the rush
off homeward via the bus.
It looks like it's going to rain,
"Thank you sir, call again"

"NEXT!"

THERE

There is a place that I do know
where flowers, lilies and water mint grow
Where cattle graze
and anglers laze,
all in the summer's glow.

Warm and sunny every day
Farmers busily making hay
Tiny insects buzzing round and round
Birds singing their joyful sound.

In this place where I can dream
sitting motionless by a stream
Endless hours, and endless days
How beautiful, this month of May.

August, July and also June
bring flowers gloriously out in bloom
Sweetened scents that fill the air
Life is peaceful, gentle, without a care.

When the summer finally ends
and nature to swallows southward send
Golden leaves fall to the ground
Northern winds whistle their lonely sound.

Long days of warmth are gone
Bitter cold will not be long
Scattered trees that sleep so bare
When the sun returns,
I'll be waiting,
THERE.....

LOVE'S DESIRE

A yearning flame, deep in my heart
begins to burn when we are apart.
Is it false, or is it real
this passionate way that I feel?

My body tingles when you are near.
I close my eyes and you are here.
You are always in my dreams
touching every nerve, it seems.

So creature of exquisite charms
let me hold you in my arms.
Smell the warm perfumed air.
To touch the softness of your hair.

To caress gently thy silky skin.
Do not disturb this dream I'm in
but come ride with me on velvet clouds
to rejoice in love, to sing out loud.

To feel happy and content
in stars and gods, that this was meant.
Is this fate or just destiny
the path that led me unto thee?

With this desire that I hold so deep
to give, but also to keep.
If time tries to take you away,
in my heart you will always stay.

DOUBT

Deep in the glade, church bells ring
  People inside cheerfully sing
    Are they happy, or am I sad?
      Are they good, or am I bad?

I stop to ponder for a while
  on my face a gentle smile
    I read the grave stones with memories upon
      loving thoughts for those who have gone.

Oh lord, why am I here!
  I shout louder, so all can hear
    A stranger looks at me, and passes by
      not wanting to stop or catch my eye.

I am a man of flesh and bone
  In a crowded world I feel alone
    What is life all about?
      I know not, I am in doubt.

But wait, in the darkness a blinding glow
  a guiding spirit, maybe to show
    the way of truth and of light
      to help me choose, wrong from right.

Oh people down there, locked in time
  you have helped me in my mind
    So I will talk to you again someday
      when I happen to pass by, this way.

IF

If I had a crown, would I be king

If I had money, would I worry about a thing

If I was a millionaire

   Would I be happy being here?

If I could stop the world, would I get off

If I talked posh, would I be a toff

If I had a car, instead of a bike

   Would I miss the things I like?

If I had no friends, would I be alone

If I had no work, would I groan

If it rained all day, without the sun

   Would it stop me having fun?

If I couldn't see, I would be sad

If I couldn't hear, I would be mad

If I couldn't talk or walk

   Would it stop me being alive?

WINDMILL SOUNDS

Windmill, windmill, spinning round
Move your stones to roaring sound
You creek and groan under strain
to turn flour from the grain.

In clouds of dust that gently air
of moving chains that do bear
the weight of sack.
Round hole and stair
the scampering feet, a hollow sound,
beating upon oak timbers, not on ground.

So men toil till work is done
from rising to setting of the sun
And when all is laid to rest
small creatures take upon the best
of wheat and chaff scattered about the floor
Searching, scurrying around for more.

Old windmill, old windmill
with sails so bare
tell me quietly of your ghosts in there
Once alive, but oh so still
Come whisper now, if that's your will.

Bricks that crack, do so tumble
In daylight you do not mumble
Still night shadows clothe your frame
Makes an image, not the same.

The wind howls and whistles clear
An awesome sight as we draw near
I feel so small, that you could crush
We flee in haste, this I must.

LUSTFUL LOVE

Oh sweet secret love of mine
I dream of you time after time.
Picturing you in my arms.
To gaze and wonder at your charms.

Oh angel with the softness of skin
open your wings and let me in.
Deep strange feelings inside are there
ever growing for me to bear.

And when my body can contain no more
the strength of feelings that soar
let's bring this passion together
for a short while, when there's not forever.

I want to kiss your secret spot
to make it sensual, soft and hot
to drift up high on a heavenly cloud
making you scream and shout out loud.

In my heart and dreams you live
keeper of these emotions to give.
Do not be afraid of what I feel
for love is wonderful, love is real.

So in my body for now, you must remain
to bear frustration, anguish and pain
until one day when it may be
I can release all my feelings into thee.

REMEMBER

Do we really need flowers to say,
Or to remind us of the day you went away,
Or to let the world see,
What you obviously meant to me?

You lay here cold and still,
A frame of bones in earth's till,
Then one day other people will pass and say,
As I beside you will lay.

They say God will judge,
Upon our errors that besmudge.
That our souls to heaven or hell,
But no one ever returns to tell.

So I place flowers your grave upon,
To remind me and others that you have gone,
I read your name written in stone,
To make us feel we're not alone.

Goodbye dear friend I must be away,
For it's not my turn as yet to stay,
I still live to have fun,
For what is my life, why it's just begun.

Yes good people standing up there,
As you look down and stare,
Enjoy your life for all it's worth,
For one day you too will inherit this earth.

THE GIFT

When summer leaves turn to autumn gold
and another year of my life has unfold
there has been so much change
that even now it feels rather strange.

Why did this happen to me?
To make blind eyes to see
a different world that I've not known
all these years that I have grown.

And as I lay there in that bed
with endless thoughts inside my head
I had time to stop and ponder
of the things overlooked and wonder.

I began to hear the birds sing,
and distant church bells ring,
the windy sounds, blowing through the trees,
and the constant humming of the bees.

The sweet fragrant scents upon the air
gifts that were always there.
How could I not be able to see
until this tragedy happened to me?

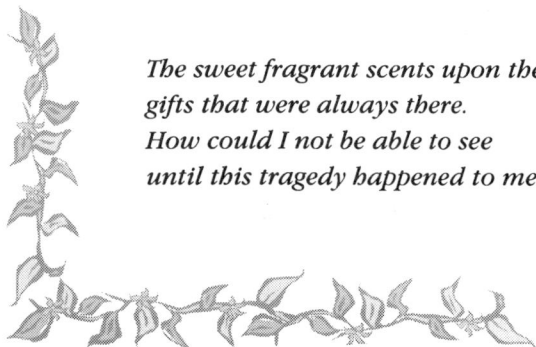

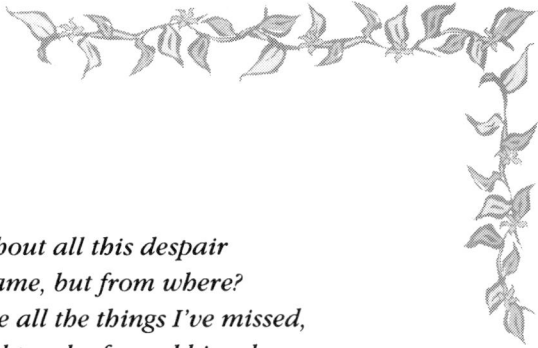

Then throughout all this despair
a stranger came, but from where?
He taught me all the things I've missed,
his voice and touch of angel kissed.

I am here for your protection
as we gaze at your mirrored reflection
so you too can walk with me
and appreciate the things I see.

To understand what is life
and to forget your tragic strife
For a positive smile rebels defiantly
And your spirit will be set free.

And so the autumn leaves do fall
As I sit in sun, shadows to recall
Whether man or angel from above
This stranger taught me to laugh, to smile, to love.

So now I know how to live
And so one day I'll return the give
The faith and strength you gave me
In my adversity.

PASSION'S LOVE

Does the grass seem greener than yesterday?
    or the love we made sweeter anyway.
Does the sky seem a different blue?
    or the world since I met you.

Do the stars twinkle more so?
    or the skylark soar higher though.
Do the flowers seem more fragrant?
    or their wafted scent more delicate.

Does the sun shimmer upon the water longer?
    or the wind blow stronger.
Does the moonlight seem more full?
    or angry storm clouds more dull.

Does the rain fall gentler upon the ground?
    or pounding waves a softer sound.
Does the spray through sunlight more glisten?
    or I in love more listen.

Does your smile broaden a happy face?
    or cause my beating pulse to race.
Does passion's love increase my desire?
    or your hair the colour of fire.

Oh yes, within my heart they do,
my dearest love because of you.
So walk with me and take my hand,
in this wonder, never land.

18

SCHOOL RENUNION

Was it so long ago
all your faces I used to know?
Then came that final day
when we said goodbye and went away.

Many things in our lives have changed,
to see you all now feels kind of strange,
but memories are always there
to remind us all for those who care.

I remember joy, laughter, sadness and tears,
as we grew up in our teenage years.
And oh, how proud we stood,
we'd rule the world if we only could.

We were so young and life was free.
Troubles came along for you and me.
Sometimes it was love, sometimes money.
We realised that growing up was not sweetness and honey.

But life through all its ups and downs
and the changes that made us frown,
we learn to cope and to adjust
as our teachers told us we must.

And what of those dear old folk
with which we used to laugh and joke.
They taught us well with good advice,
though I, like many, sometimes needed telling twice.

As I look around at you all tonight,
your happy faces makes my world feel right.
I salute you and my regards I send,
Cheers, God bless, and to absent friends......

THESE NOBLY PLAYED THEIR PART

POPPY DAY

I am a flower of scarlet red,
With my flimsy floppy head,
Blowing freely in the wind,
A remembrance symbol to those who sinned.

And on a November's day,
Memories and reminders people say,
To honour those who are dead,
A ring of moss, filled with stricken heads.

There I'm placed by royal Kings and Queens,
Beneath statues, for all is seen,
To make us think and remember so,
Those poor souls to battle go.

Ne'r to return to family and friends,
For in those muddy bloody fields did end,
We did not know of torture or of stricken foe,
Do we really care! I suppose so.

For here we stand proud to honour thee,
Unknown names that set us free,
We appreciate your sacrifice on this day,
To remind us all to say .... THANK YOU ....

OLD MAN'S THOUGHTS

Thinking back to when I was a lad,
of all the things I never had
Times, I've seen so much change,
that nothing ever remains the same
There was I, three sisters, two brothers,

> *Put another log on the fire mother.*

There was never a lot to eat,
and we hardly ever tasted meat
Father worked hard in his own way,
though it was never worth the pay
But live we did, for each day,

> *Put another log on the fire mother.*

In the Autumn we could wear a grin,
for that's when the fishing fleet comes in
Brown bread, butter and herring for tea
Blast they tasted good and I ate three,
With my contented tum, and my father sipping rum,

> *Put another log on the fire mother.*

The winters I remember were very cold
It was hard for us young 'uns, but worse for the old
Still if help was needed friends would gather round
A morsel here, a morsel there, something would soon be found
We were all poor but happy in sound,

> *Put another log on the fire mother.*

Three score and ten in Yarmouth town,
I bow my head and wear a frown
Through my eyes I see this day,
Changes that come, but what can I say
Most are bad, but some are good
I do it different if I could,

   Put another log on the fire mother.

Now I'm old and mind does stray
My hair is also turning grey
The world outside, is not a happy one
There is no contentment in the young
They have more possessions, that is true
They do not value the things I do

   Put another log on the fire mother.

It's nice and cosy by my fire
If I said I'd been a saint, well I'd be a liar
I think I've had a happy life, with my children and little wife
Love's path is never smooth, sometimes I was downright rude,
and I've never run wild in the nude

   Put another log on the fire mother.

Oh well, wishful thinking that's what's left for me
I am not as sprightly as I used to be
Still I'm healthy and happy and that's a lot
This fire ain't aft bloody hot,

   Put another log on the fire, MOTHER ....

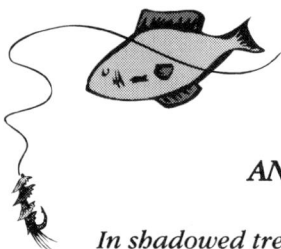

ANGLER'S JOY

In shadowed trees that grow so tall
live creatures of the night, some large some small.
Every sound is eerie and clear,
echoing loudly in my ear.

In the night to catch a fish.
There's my cast, the sound a swish.
A gentle plop reveals my flake,
as it settles upon the lake.

There's a gulp, a suck and then a slurp.
Quietly now, do not disturb.
A mighty splash, and then I feel
the line flying from my reel.

Swiftly up to strike the hook
in the darkness the creature took.
First to the left and then to the right,
to gain its freedom, the fish must fight.

Under strain my line does sing.
Slowly to net the carp I bring.
Happiness and joy soon fills my heart.
A brief encounter and then to part.

A chance to savour this passage in time.
Distant church bells start to chime.
The night has gone and day is born.
All too soon it will be dawn.

A WEDDING POEM

I hear church bells ringing loud,
See family and friends standing proud,
We to witness and hear you swear,
You devoted love to declare.

To the marriage that you make,
Don't forget to give and take,
A blessed future of happiness,
Based on care and thoughtfulness.

Words of wisdom in every way,
Leaves only one thing to say,
Good luck, God bless,
Have a nice day ....

FRIENDS

Friends are people who think of you
Friends are people with nice things to do
When you are lonely does anybody care?
And you wonder if there's someone out there.

Then oh!, to my surprise
you brought tears to my eyes
Flowers, chocolates and a smiling face,
makes the world a better place
A lump in my throat, a beat in my heart
All the time there when we were apart.

You are the greatest friends to me,
and in return, I to thee,
A sweaty palm, a crimpled bank,
With the warmest and sincerest
Thanks.

A WOODLAND VIEW

Through woodlands I walk on a winter's dawn,
Vibrant sun glistens upon a dewdrop thorn,
Small birds hurriedly searching for food,
Intensifies nature's mystic mood.

Light cascades down through silhouetted trees,
Fire smoke drifting silently on the breeze,
Evergreen holly, ivy and yew,
Embraces my path that I walk through.

A squirrel sleeps snug in his leafy drey,
As quietly slips by another motionless day,
Cock pheasants showing off kaleidoscopic feathers,
Delicate snowdrops, primroses and fragrant heathers.

Dormant boughs that slumber bare,
Bathed in beams of shimmering glare,
Of fallen leaves that carpet wooded ground,
A robin shrills its melodious territorial sound.

Restless pigeons with ever watching eye,
Alarms the wood as I pass by,
The wren vocals his annoyance with musical adorn,
As my amblings intrude on nature's dawn.

And so the return of warm days, albeit slowly,
Rising misty clouds, their shapes appearing ghostly,
Dispersed angry tormented skies of grey,
Brings forth a flawless blue on another day.

Restored life to creatures in hibernated sleep,
Crystal icicles begin to weep,
And to rivers once again do torrents flow,
Springs return will energetically grow.

Distant cold frost, snow and winds,
As the earth's impoverished season ends,
Observed days elongated by time,
The sun strengthens an imaginative mind.

A TRAMP'S WAY

The sky is my roof
and the mother earth my bed.
A log or a rock my pillow,
is where I lay my head.

> *I care not for cars, lorries or bikes,*
> *for these are not the things I like,*
> *but the birds and bees,*
> *gentle breezes, flowers and trees.*

A world destined far apart,
from that what's in your beating heart.
For I like the simple way
as endlessly I stroll each day.

> *For what is life, in your mind*
> *Not for me the material kind,*
> *rushing here, rushing there*
> *but never ever getting WHERE!*

I take only what I need
in this life to succeed.
I may not look to you so well
and at times I guess I smell.

> *My clothes are not neat and trim*
> *and I never wear fashion's whim*
> *I don't possess posh shoes*
> *or hanker to eat in fancy muse.*

I do not have clean shiny hair,
or anyone else for me to care.
But then all I need is me,
for I am a person who is free.

> *I have no agenda, no real direction,*
> *but an infinitive time for reflection.*
> *A lane today, tomorrow a road,*
> *wherever life takes me, it's my home.*

A DYING WISH

I wish I could walk in a rainy day
feel upon my face the ocean spray
to stroll along the beach when the wind blow
do all sorts of things if I had known.

I wish I could listen to the little birds' song
when I ambled slowly along
and sit awhile in the scented air
of warm summer days without a care.

I wished I'd walked instead of run
to be glad and too had fun
as I imagine the clouds drifting by
in an ever changing sky.

I wish I could do the little things
gaze at birds that hover on tiny wings
but here I lay also still
my body no longer has the will.

I wish I wasn't deaf and could have heard
and that my sight wasn't so blurred
and my words were not so slurred
for in my speech I dribble

I wish I ....

SOLDIER'S RETURN

The training barracks where soldiers live
And when to war their lives must give
A call to arms, here we go
To defeat the aggressive foe.

With tank, canon, rifle and gun
Will not end till battles won
Some of them will have to die
And friends and family when told, will cry.

But we are honour bound
Sworn to defend this sacred ground
And to spill our life's blood
For this land which we love.

Many of our enemies are unknown
And in pain and agony we groan
When in conflict we will fear
And think of those we hold so dear.

If I am lucky to return
We will remember those poor souls who burned
For it is against God's will
My fellow man to kill

But the sun shines on another day
With medals and wreaths we honour this way
For those who were brave
Who gave so not to enslave.

And as I sit here to think
Slowly sipping a mellow drink
A crunchy bite from marmalade toast

I SURVIVED.

MY WORLD

You are as beautiful as the morning sunrise
and the starlight that twinkles in your eyes
is as sweet as spring scent upon the breeze
and the rustling wind through leaved trees.

Like a harmonious melody of a bird's song,
sonic notes, short and long
but joyfully in tune.
Warm sultry nights in June.

Of owls that shriek their eerie call.
As cute as foxes when small.
You are gentle as the rain
and the earthy smell of grain.

I know not if you were heaven sent,
or fate chosen this as meant.
Do all angels have wings
or say angelic things?

All this and more in you I see,
and the happiness you made in me.
So let nature's secrets unfurl
for my sweetest love, you are my world.

MEMORIES

I, an old man sits on a cliff top bench and watches the sea
and reminisces about how things used to be.
The waves pounding upon the shore,
small sanderlings scurrying about for more.

Oh the sea, it was my life.
More important and tempestuous than a wife.
Its many changing moods
and its harsh treatment of fools.

What makes you so, the moon, the earth, I suppose.
I don't expect we well ever know,
for you are a wonder of this world
and your secrets only slowly unfurl.

I've seen you angry with mighty waves,
an awesome power to enslave,
and who chooses who to die
and those lucky to see another sky.

But then on another day
you amble on in a motionless way.
Your salty spray soft upon my face,
and dolphins playfully skipping in the bow race.

But never forget that watchful eye
as gulls shriek their ever hungry cry.
You bring a wild spirit from within
to a seaman's face, a laugh, a grin.

My body still pitches and rolls to your rhythm,
a lesson learnt but which never given.
I walk even now on land with a gentle sway
as I stroll down to this bench every day.

Oh how I love thee, and I still can
because I'm just a retired old man.
"What are you watching?", a youngster asks me.
"Just the sea lad, just the sea".

CREATION

Did God really make the earth,
precious gifts, gold, frankincense and mirth?
He gave his only son
to teach us all to love someone.

We rejoice and celebrate at Christmas time
beside a flickering candled flame, to remind,
to reminisce about the things we need,
to forget life's material greed.

To caress, cherish and love,
teachings of our lord above,
that we one day will be humble and wise,
and to show an honesty, not disguised.

Oh reach out thy peoples' hand.
Believe in me and understand.
Be kind, gentle and sincere.
Gifts beholdeth man, bestowed my dear.

And through the holiest of books
upon my creation, widened eyes will look.
Peaceful worlds, perfection apart,
giftful from the bottom of my heart.

Teaching Christ's message, disciples did go.
To love thy neighbour and toil, so
that one day our children will see.
To all creeds I forgive thee.

And when the day you cometh to me,
Angels of light sent to guide, be
Your spirit beside me siteth on high
Then OH then, will you not Deny.

TINTAGEL

King Arthur, Guinevere and Lancelot
A ring of knights called Camelot
Strong and pure as the driven snow
A wizard and a magic sword
All those romantic years ago.

I touch your battle scarred walls
How many men have you witnessed fall?
A cut with a sword, a thrust of a lance
Neither given them a second chance.

As men scream in anger and pain
Your seemingless flint expression remains
Many fall to their knees, others to battle ground
Forever still, no more a sound.

Drawing closer I can hear the victory won
As you watch the enemy run
A silent arrow still finds its mark
Released true from the bowman's arch.

But what of victorious celebration and dance
Time enough for joy, lust and romance
To drink the ale and take thy fill
Telling of stories enlarged at will.

And so to sleep for contented souls
But what of dead friends, comrades and fools
For thy king they did obey
Not ever to return another day.

As the blood dries in the morning sun
Again and again song, merriment and fun
But remain the stones, a silent witness to it all
When will you again watch them fall?

As I stand before you dwarfed alone
Of mayhem fire and brimstone
I shudder as I recall
Beneath this cold ancient wall........

BARGAIN DAY

Up early with the lark
to find a place for the car to park.
Credit cards and money, so we can pay
on our bargain shopping day.

    Park and ride to catch the bus
    so when in town there's no rush.
    A crowd of people filling every store.
    Expectant hunters on each shop floor.

Some prefer diamond jewellery or golden rings,
others clothes and alternative things.
Round and round excitedly on every street,
not wanting to stop or old friends to greet.

    People with delighted smiling faces,
    as they visit many strange places.
    Knick knacks, records, pictures, clothes and shoes
    as they all buzz around the shopping muse.

Swipe, swipe, ring, as the money rolls in.
Shopkeeper and customer with contented grin.
Coloured bags and parcels all brim full.
Life is fast, on the pulse, and never dull.

    And so we stop briefly for a bite to eat.
    Tea, coffee to drink and a pause for aching feet.
    A casual smile and a nod for someone we know.
    Can't be offensive, we'll just say "Hello".

Courteously speaking, "Having a nice day"
as we gradually keep on walking away.
Then in this melee, shrieking mobile phones
with all their multi lingual ring tones.

Guys and girls looking in the mirror to see
Whether this or that will suit me.
A delicate moment of pretty lace
brings a flirtatious smile from a cheeky face.

Shops for women, shops for men,
bright and delightful, lets pop in, then
rushing in giving everything a glance,
not particularly looking, only something by chance.

Coloured garments of green, red, yellow and blue,
picked up, tossed around, all are new.
Some for the summer, some for now.
It's too small, no it will fit somehow.

With laden and bulging arms, aching so.
Catch the bus, it's time to go.
It takes a while to get on its way.
Upon reflection it's been a nice happy day.

SECRET PASSIONS

You seem a stranger to me
though I call you friend.
So may I dance with thee
until the music ends.

The sound is slow and smooth,
locked we are in rhythmic mood.
Bodies swaying gently to and fro,
ever tighter, don't let go.

We glide as one across the floor,
each step in timely dance,
lost in the music forever more,
together in love's trance.

I feel your body and wafts of scented air.
Eyes gaze but we are not aware,
for we are drifting on a heavenly cloud.
The music softer, not so loud.

On and on the melody play,
and onward our mind does stray,
swept away on a motions tide.
Deep loves feelings we cannot hide.

If only I could stop the world
and capture this moment in time,
to feel your arms around me,
but never to be mine.

All too soon the music fades.
Time for you to go away.
One last moment to steal a kiss.
Is it a stranger or a friend, that I will miss?

DEATH

O people with sadden faces
    waiting in this mournful of places,
        gazing at my empty shell
            where my spirits no longer dwell.

Gone is the passion, the spark of life
    from my body of torment and strife.
        No time to look back with regret,
            no sorrow to forgive, no memory to forget.

I can no longer do what's not been done.
    I cannot laugh or have fun.
        My life here was full of joy,
            although sometimes I got annoyed.

My time has come to pass you by,
    to journey with an all seeing eye,
        to a place of paradise and friendliness,
            welcomed by souls with warm caress.

I take not with me possessions or so,
    for I my spirit alone must go
        to a place reserved in the sky
            to sit beside my God on high.

I look back one last time
    of friends and family that were mine.
        Goodbye, farewell as you remain
            I await in heaven till we meet again.

ANNIVERSARY SONG

Was it really 25 years ago,
to a person who I didn't know
I got on bended knee
and beg you to marry me?

There were doubts, you told me so
and you didn't really want to go,
but destiny has its way
and as we see, you did stay.

Then came along our little boy
that filled my heart full of joy.
He had a happy smiling face
and made my world a wonderful place.

A year or more and then a girl,
not a lot of hair but she had curls.
Little angels as they lay asleep.
Now my family was complete.

And as old Father Time rolled on by,
sometimes we would argue, sometimes cry.
Life is full of ups and downs,
and situations that make us frown.

But through all the thick and thin,
shoulder to the wheel, and all pitch in,
and after all the screams and shout,
we would sit down and work it out.

Over the years we learn to change
because nothing ever remains the same,
but there's one thing that's always true,
the love in my heart for you.

So looking back at our life,
"Thank you my dear, it's been nice".

TRAVEL

Do we ever realise how lucky we are
to travel distances near and far
by boat, car, motorbike or train
and across continents by jet plane.

Wonderful achievements of the human race
to sit and think our kind went into space
then eventually walked on the moon
and then came back, anointed heroes to swoon.

We can hover above the ground
airless suspension no wires to be found.
When one day we will get it right
and fly like birds in effortless flight.

Oh we have lived in exciting times
that have inquisitive, inventive minds.
For what mindful man can conceive,
the body will eventually achieve.

Unfulfilled cravings will increase hunger's need
for even greater intensive speed.
Well now I agree, it seems a bit potty
but one day we will say,

"BEAM ME UP SCOTTY

WORK DAY

I awoke in a violent haze,
as my alarm clock hailed another day.
Sleepy, stumbled from my bed
with an ever fuzzy head.

Advancing the bathroom to shower and shave,
smartly to dress, we must behave.
A small breakfast, not a morsel more,
then I marched briskly out the door.

I viewed a chap reading a book,
looked peaceful enough,
a woman walking her dog, picking up its stuff.
Happy in their way,
Who am I to say?

The sky was blue with not a cloud.
The sun shone, birds sung sweetly out loud.
Cars roared and snarled stuck in endless jams.
I was dreaming of fields with playful lambs.

A blasting horn brought me back
to reality. That's where I sat
in a car, in a jam, what a fact.
Then across my path strolled a black shiny cat.

A lucky day it was to be,
me and all the others that did see.
Why do I have to work and labour so,
with aching limbs and bones? But still I go.

Ever onward through this drudgery
in endless pursuit of the coin, money.
If I was rich would it be the same?
I suppose it would, it's all a game.

Oh well here we are, back again.
Perhaps later it might rain.
"Work!" shouts the boss, "I want profit, not loss"
"Don't we....." "What did you say?......" "Nothing"
A sly grin and a rebellious smirk.
Just another day at work

UFO

A burning question, the answer we don't know,
the unexplained mystery of the UFO.
The government police and army all deny
what thousands have witnessed in the sky.

Do they think we are so naïve
that our intelligence cannot conceive
that there could be people from another planet
And we are not alone on this piece of granite?

An odd bright light burning bright
as it flashes across the universal night.
Does it keep flying or will it land?
If it does will we understand?

For something we refused to recognise
may one day confront us and materialise.
Then will the forces massively deploy
loads of men and weapons to destroy?

Will we stretch out a hand and be friend,
or be apprehensive and just defend?
Controlling our fear and not just to kill
but to embrace the spectacle and the thrill.

Who knows, they could teach us to learn
about cancers, diseases; answers we yearn
to make this world of ours a better place
for all the people of the human race.

So before uncertainty chooses to condemn
those strangers that may help to mend,
let's take breath and ponder awhile
at the amazing prospect, and smile

For they in return may think us strange
because we kill, torture, destroy; are we not deranged?
So contemplate earth people just a moment or so
the next time you gaze at a UFO.

AUSCHWITZ

Of all the millions that were forcefully slaughtered,
Fathers, Brothers, Sons, Mothers, Sisters and Daughters.
Stench filled smoke rising in the sky
as those poor souls went to die.

Enforcers of honour, NO, perpetrators of evil.
Manipulated beings that were weak and feeble.
They held no shame, no remorse
as they pursued their wretched course.

Inhuman, and to hide their vileness deeds
did burn and bury many innocent creeds,
but this was a monumental holocaust
destined in history to be scorched.

So we must never ever let
the passing of time to erode and forget.
For I bow my head in shame
although all people were not to blame.

So contemplate! we as a human race
could ever build such a place
and then lead people there to die in fear
blind and deaf to crying merciful tears.

And to the criminal, justice was not done.
No victory celebrations, no battle won,
but revenge and anger in a nation's heart
for all those people that took part.

Come the day of judgement and retribution
those cowards ran and hid from prosecution,
pretending and denying "it was not I,
We weren't involved with those to die".

Some captured leaders of the S.S. gang
unrepented, trialled and hanged.
But only one's life, was that repay
for all the thousands that died each day?

Yes, reflect in astonishment from time to time
and never, never, ever fail to remind
the race of people that did that stuff
just saying "SORRY " I'm afraid is not good ENOUGH.

DOCTORS

Sitting in the doctor's surgery,
feverish, fatigued and downright poorly.
The receptionist cries "Mr B.
You're up next, the Doc. will see".

A colourful tank of tropical fish
and a delightful ornamental dish,
a vase of flowers out in bloom,
to try and brighten up the gloom.

I look around at the other people here
waiting patiently, from who knows where,
to see if there's someone I've known,
while listening to all the coughs and groans.

She doesn't look ill, nor does he,
so what are you doing here, beside me?
Wasting all the medic's time
making my wait, longer in line.

"I'm ill. I'm ill, can't you see?"
a young girl tries to convince me.
Your appearance doesn't so relate,
whispering it's best, if you didn't wait.

Look at her over there
dressed up mutton with fancy hair.
Every day here, in that flimsy frock.
She's smitten and got a crush on the Doc.

Oh! there he is in his pure white coat,
stethoscope draped round his neck, the old goat.
Who does he think he is?
Delightful, "You're next, please miss".

Hey wait a minute! I was here before,
as I angrily pace across the floor.
"Sorry sir, there's been a bit of a mix
Could you possibly come back at six?"

Oh yes, you'd like to wish.
I've been waiting three days for this.
So why don't you just give me a pill?
"No I cannot Sir, are you really ill?"

Eventually I get the nod
and then the medic starts to prod.
"Where does it hurt, you didn't say so?"
Well Doc. how am I supposed to know?

"I can't find anything wrong.
Have you been suffering long?
I'll give you a note just for a week
although I think you have got a cheek".

Thank you, I'm feeling a bit better right now.
"Ah I thought you would some how".
Well Doc. it's true what they say
"Yes Sir, have a nice day".

47

MOTORBIKE

Gleaming, engineered and precision made,
a racing motorcycle called a Fireblade.
Designed perfection, built for speed
for all those who feel the need.

I start the engine, roar, roar, roar
as the beast screams out, more, more, more.
Releasing the clutch and then I feel
the awesome power from machine to wheel.

Scream, scream, scream, faster, faster, faster,
mind alert, body tingling, avoiding disaster.
I feel exhilarated, and excitement in my bones
as every gear change alters engine tones.

This is man's passion and unsatisfied greed.
His love affair with ultimate speed.
For even though we're told to slow
it's ignored and we don't want to know.

For astride this rocket I am king.
Passing every sluggish thing.
Fizzing down straights, whizzing round corners,
passing open mouthed admirers, and waving adorers.

130 - 140 - 150 - one hundred and sixty,
as the bike becomes even more thrifty.
Taking off like a jet propelled manned missile.
The power unbelievable, alluring and beguile.

And so, finally once more we are still.
Silently reliving the speeding thrill.
For now it's time for me to clean
and you to become once more just a gleaming machine.

There my beast, be still your beating heart
for we are never very far apart
because when I sit on you astride
we become as one,
                    ALIVE............